SHETLAND VISITORS GUIDE 2024

A Straightforward Guidebook on Everything You Need to Do and Know about Exploring Shetland, UK

LARA BILL

Copyright©2024 Lara Bill

All Rights Reserved

INTRODUCTION

PART 1: UNWRAPPING SHETLAND - BEYOND PUFFINS AND PONIES

CHAPTER 1: SHETLAND UNSCRIPTED:
1.1 A TAPESTRY WOVEN THROUGH TIME
1.2 BEYOND THE SHETLANDSCAPE
1.3 NAVIGATING YOUR ISLAND VOYAGE
CHAPTER 2: LERWICK - SHETLAND'S VIBRANT HEART
2.1 FROM HANSEATIC CHARM TO MODERN MARVELS
Lerwick Town Hall: A Gateway to Hanseatic Heritage
2.2 MUSEUMS & ART GALLERIES
Shetland Museum and Archives
Bonhoga Gallery

PART 2: MAINLAND MAGIC - UNVEILING SHETLAND'S CROWN JEWELS

CHAPTER 3: SCALLOWAY & JARLSHOF
3.1 SCALLOWAY CASTLE
3.2 JARLSHOF - A PREHISTORIC PLAYGROUND
3.3 MOUSA BROCH: IRON AGE ENIGMA
CHAPTER 4: SUMBURGH HEAD & BEYOND
4.1 SUMBURGH HEAD - NATURE'S WONDERLAND
Sumburgh Head
4.2 SHETLAND'S WILD WEST
Fitful Head
4.3 MUCKLE FLUGGA LIGHTHOUSE
Muckle Flugga Lighthouse
CHAPTER 5: MAINLAND DELIGHTS: QUAINT VILLAGES, SCENIC DRIVES, AND HIDDEN GEMS
5.1 VOE VILLAGES

Voe Villages
5.2 SCENIC DRIVES & ISLAND HIGHLIGHTS
Exploring Mainland's Rugged Beauty
Discovering Standing Stones
Picnic by Hidden Lochs
5.3 BEYOND THE TOURIST TRAIL
Secret Beaches and Hidden Coves
Quaint Craft Shops and Artisanal Finds
Authentic Pubs and Local Hangouts

PART 3: ISLAND HOPPING: UNVEILING SHETLAND'S HIDDEN TREASURES

CHAPTER 6: BRESSAY & WHALSAY
6.1 BRESSAY - AN ISLAND OASIS
Bressay Island Oasis
6.2 WHALSAY - WHERE HISTORY SLEEPS
Whalsay Island Serenity
CHAPTER 7: UNST & YELL
7.1 UNST - UNTAMED BEAUTY
7.2 YELL - BIRDWATCHER'S HAVEN
Yell - A Symphony of Wings
CHAPTER 8: FETLAR & PAPA STOUR
8.1 FETLAR - ISLAND OF CONTRASTS
Fetlar - A Tapestry of Nature and History
8.2 PAPA STOUR - A TRANQUIL RETREAT
Papa Stour - A Haven of Solitude

PART 4: EXPERIENCING SHETLAND

CHAPTER 9: ADVENTURES AT SEA
9.1 EXPLORE HIDDEN COVES & SEA CAVES
Sea Kayaking Shetland - A Watery Wonderland

9.2 SURF'S UP!
Shetland Surf School - Ride the Waves of the North Atlantic
9.3 SAILING THE SHETLANDSCAPE
Shetland Yachting - Sail into the Sunset
CHAPTER 10: ON LAND & FOOT
10.1 HIKING HIGHLANDS & MOORLANDS
The Cliff Path
Rona Hill
Bein Nibba National Scenic Area
10.2 PEDAL THROUGH HISTORY & NATURE
The Mainland Trail
Hidden Paths by the Sea
10.3 SHETLAND PONIES & GENTLE TRAILS
CHAPTER 11: ARTS & CULTURE
11.1 PEERIE FESTIVALS & LOCAL TALENT
Shetland Folk Festival - A Melodic Tapestry of Traditions
11.2 CRAFT & TRADITION
11.3 UP-HELLY-AA FIRE FESTIVAL
Up-Helly-Aa Festival - Flames of Viking Heritage

PART 6: SHETLAND FOR EVERY SEASON

CHAPTER 12: CHOOSING YOUR ADVENTURE: FROM SUMMER SUN TO WINTER WONDERS
12.1 MIDNIGHT SUN & WILDLIFE WATCHING
12.2 AUTUMN FOLIAGE & COZY COMFORT
12.3 WINTER LANDSCAPES & NORTHERN LIGHTS
CHAPTER 13: ESSENTIAL INFORMATION & PRACTICAL TIPS FOR ADVENTURERS
13.1 GETTING HERE & GETTING AROUND
13.2: SHETLAND'S FINEST HOTELS
13.3 BUDGETING & PACKING WISELY

Introduction

Ah, Shetland! The wind whispers Viking tales against your face, sea spray paints rainbows on the air, and sheep graze on cliffs the color of ancient dreams. My time there wasn't just a trip; it was an initiation into a wild, windswept world.

Imagine this: I stood on Sumburgh Head, where the North Sea crashes against cliffs teeming with guillemots, puffins, and razorbills. The wind tried to snatch my hat, but laughter was stronger, echoing across the moors. Beneath me, seals sunned themselves on black rocks, oblivious to the drama above.

Later, I wandered through Lerwick, its colorful houses huddled like fishermen's tales under a sky smeared with sunset. The scent of freshly baked oatcakes drifted from cozy cafes, and the pubs brimmed with the lilt of Shetland Scots, stories woven as intricately as the local knitwear.

One day, I hopped on a ferry to Bressay, where time felt delightfully stuck in a slower gear. I explored Broch of Clickimin, a prehistoric puzzle of stone whispers, imagining Pictish lives lived millennia ago. Later, I picnicked on a hidden beach, the sand warm under my fingers, the ocean a turquoise jewel framed by towering cliffs.

But Shetland wasn't just about scenery, it was about people. I learned to knit like a local, my clumsy fingers guided by patient hands that had spun tales through generations. I shared a dram of peaty whisky with a crofter whose stories were etched on his face like the lines on the hills. In their warmth and resilience, I saw the soul of Shetland reflected.

Finally, I stood under the star-dusted dome of a Shetland night. The Northern Lights, ethereal curtains of emerald and amethyst, danced across the sky, a celestial ballet whispered into existence by the wind. At that moment, I felt small, connected to something larger than myself, a speck in the vast symphony of nature.

Shetland wasn't just a beautiful place, it was a feeling. It was the thrill of exploring the unknown, the comfort of a crackling peat fire, the joy of a shared story, the raw beauty of nature whispering its secrets. It was a place where time slowed down, where worries dissolved like mist in the wind, and where the spirit soared as free as the seabirds on the cliffs.

So, if you're looking for an adventure that will stir your soul, Shetland awaits. Pack your boots, your hat, and a heart open to the wild. Go, listen to the wind, and let Shetland unravel its magic before you.

Part 1: Unwrapping Shetland - Beyond Puffins and Ponies

Chapter 1: Shetland Unscripted:

Welcome to the untamed beauty of Shetland, where every craggy coastline and gentle moor whispers tales of a rich history woven through time. In this chapter, we'll embark on a journey to unravel Shetland's past, explore its diverse landscapes, and chart a course for your island adventure.

1.1 A Tapestry Woven through Time

Shetland Museum and Archives

Address: Hay's Dock, Lerwick, Shetland, ZE1 0WP, United Kingdom

Contact: +44 1595 695057

Website: www.shetlandmuseumandarchives.org.uk

Step into the Shetland Museum and Archives, a cultural sanctuary nestled in Lerwick. Here, the island's history unfolds like a vivid tapestry, chronicling the sagas of Vikings, the enigmatic presence of Picts, and the resilient spirit that defines modern Shetland.

Opening its doors daily from 10 am to 5 pm, the museum offers an immersive experience for a nominal fee of around £8. As you traverse through time, consider joining a guided tour to delve deeper into the narratives behind artifacts like Viking longships and Pictish stones. Engage with passionate guides who breathe life into Shetland's storied past.

To make the most of your visit, don't rush through; take your time absorbing the intricate details of each exhibit. The museum's café provides a delightful spot to reflect, offering locally brewed tea or coffee and panoramic views of Lerwick's picturesque harbor.

1.2 Beyond the Shetlandscape

Guided Nature Walk - Hermaness National Nature Reserve

Address: Unst, Shetland, ZE2 9DL, United Kingdom

Contact: +44 1463 667600

Website: www.nature.scot

Immerse yourself in the untouched beauty of Hermaness National Nature Reserve on the island of Unst. A guided nature walk through this reserve is a poetic journey through dramatic cliffs, seabird colonies, and expansive moors.

For an approximate fee of £18, experienced guides will lead you through marked trails, such as the cliff-top path to the iconic Muckle Flugga lighthouse. Ensure you book in advance, especially during the summer months (May to August) when puffins and other seabirds grace the skies.

Wear comfortable, weather-appropriate clothing and sturdy hiking boots. Bring a pair of binoculars to marvel at the diverse birdlife that calls Hermaness home. The best times for birdwatching are early mornings and late evenings, adding a touch of magic to your nature encounter.

1.3 Navigating Your Island Voyage

Island Hopping Adventure - Shetland Islands Council Ferries

Address: Shetland Islands Council, 8 North Ness Business Park, Lerwick, Shetland, ZE1 0LZ, United Kingdom

Contact: +44 1595 693535

Website: www.shetland.gov.uk/ferries

Embark on a maritime escapade with Shetland Islands Council Ferries, setting sail from Lerwick Ferry Terminal. This island-hopping adventure allows you to explore both the Mainland's highlights and the unique character of neighboring islands.

Ferry costs vary, with an average round-trip fee to islands like Whalsay or Bressay being around £12. Plan your trip based on the ferry schedules, which may change seasonally. For an immersive experience, consider a multi-day adventure, hopping between islands and absorbing their individual charm.

To optimize your journey, check the weather forecast before setting sail, as Shetland's weather can be unpredictable. Be open to spontaneous discoveries, and don't hesitate to engage with locals for insider tips on hidden gems along your island-hopping route.

As you navigate the uncharted waters of Shetland, let the spirit of the islands guide you to experiences that transcend stereotypes, embracing the raw and authentic essence of this mesmerizing archipelago.

Chapter 2: Lerwick - Shetland's Vibrant Heart

2.1 From Hanseatic Charm to Modern Marvels

Lerwick Town Hall: A Gateway to Hanseatic Heritage

- **Address:** Lerwick Town Hall, Commercial St, Lerwick, Shetland, ZE1 0HB, United Kingdom

- **Contact:** +44 1595 744511

- **Website:** www.shetland.gov.uk/lerwick-town-hall/visit-town-hall

Begin your Lerwick adventure at the Lerwick Town Hall, a towering symbol of Hanseatic heritage. Nestled on Commercial Street, this architectural masterpiece mirrors the town's historic ties with the Hanseatic League. As you enter, the maritime allure unfolds, with relics and artifacts echoing tales of trade and seafaring adventures.

Open to visitors Monday to Friday from 9 am to 5 pm, the Town Hall offers a captivating journey through time, and entry is free. To maximize your experience, consider joining one of the guided tours offered by knowledgeable local guides. These tours, often starting at 11 am, provide a deeper understanding of Lerwick's evolution, from a quaint trading post to a thriving maritime hub.

As you explore, take a moment to appreciate the blend of old-world charm and contemporary vibrancy that defines Commercial Street. Quaint shops, traditional pubs, and the lively buzz of locals create an ambiance that seamlessly fuses the town's rich history with its modern identity.

Getting the Most Out of Lerwick Town Hall:

- **Guided Tours:** Engage with the local guides who share anecdotes and hidden gems that might escape the untrained eye.

- **Cafés and Shops:** Take a stroll along Commercial Street, popping into the charming cafes and shops that line the route. Don't rush; let the town unfold at its own pace.

- **Waterfront Views:** Head towards the waterfront for panoramic views of Lerwick's bustling harbor. The changing tides and boat activity add a dynamic layer to your experience.

Lerwick Town Hall Summary:

Average Cost: Free entry; Guided tours approximately £5-£8 per person

Opening Times: Monday to Friday, 9 am to 5 pm; Guided tours usually start at 11 am

Directions: Located on Commercial Street, Lerwick; easily accessible on foot from the town center

Amenities: Nearby cafes, shops, and waterfront views

Embark on this journey through Lerwick's maritime past at the Town Hall, where every step echoes with the whispers of centuries-old stories.

Next stop: Museums & Art Galleries - where shipwrecks, Pictish mysteries, and local artistic talent converge in Lerwick's cultural tapestry.

2.2 Museums & Art Galleries

Shetland Museum and Archives

- **Address:** Hay's Dock, Lerwick, Shetland, ZE1 0WP, United Kingdom

- **Contact:** +44 1595 695057

- **Website:** www.shetlandmuseumandarchives.org.uk

Nestled on the edge of Hay's Dock, the Shetland Museum and Archives beckons history enthusiasts and curious wanderers alike. This cultural haven opens its doors daily from 10 am to 5 pm, welcoming you to embark on a maritime journey through Shetland's past.

The Maritime Story: Dive into the maritime heritage of Shetland as you explore artifacts from shipwrecks, fishing traditions, and the island's enduring connection with the sea. The museum's layout, designed to be immersive, allows you to step back in time and witness the evolution of Lerwick from a Viking outpost to a modern hub.

Guided Tours: Enhance your museum experience by joining one of the guided tours, usually starting around 11 am. Knowledgeable guides weave tales of Viking sagas and the island's resilience, providing a deeper understanding of the exhibits.

Café Overlooking the Harbor: Take a break at the museum's café, strategically positioned to offer breathtaking views of Lerwick's harbor. Savor a cup of locally brewed tea or coffee while reflecting on the island's layered history.

Additional Events and Workshops: Check the museum's schedule for special events, lectures, and workshops that provide a more immersive exploration of Shetland's culture. Engage with experts and fellow enthusiasts to gain a deeper appreciation for the island's rich tapestry.

Average Cost: Approximately £8 per person (free entry for children under 16)

Opening Times: Daily from 10 am to 5 pm; Guided tours typically start at 11 am

Directions: Located on Hay's Dock, accessible by foot from the town center

Amenities: Café, gift shop, guided tours, events, workshops

Venture beyond the artifacts; let the Shetland Museum and Archives be your time-traveling vessel, navigating the currents of history with every exhibit.

Bonhoga Gallery

- **Address:** Weisdale Mill, Weisdale, Shetland, ZE2 9LW, United Kingdom

- **Contact:** +44 1595 745750

- **Website:** www.shetlandarts.org/venues/bonhoga

- For those with an appreciation for contemporary art, the Bonhoga Gallery, situated in Weisdale Mill, is a feast for the senses. Open from Tuesday to Sunday, 11 am to 4 pm, this gallery showcases the diverse talents of local and international artists against the backdrop of Shetland's rugged beauty.

Artistic Diversity: Immerse yourself in a collection that spans various mediums and styles, celebrating the creative spirit of Shetland. From paintings and sculptures to installations, each piece tells a story that resonates with the island's untamed landscape.

Temporary Exhibitions: Explore the dynamic nature of the gallery through its temporary exhibitions, which change periodically. Check the gallery's schedule for information on ongoing and upcoming exhibits, adding an element of surprise to your visit.

Average Cost: Approximately £5 per person (concessions available)

Opening Times: Tuesday to Sunday, 11 am to 4 pm

Directions: Located in Weisdale Mill; accessible by car or public transport from Lerwick

Amenities: Gift shop, artistic workshops, temporary exhibitions

Bonhoga Gallery is more than a static display; it's a living canvas that captures the essence of Shetland's creative heartbeat. Let the brushstrokes and installations guide you through a sensory exploration of contemporary expression.

Part 2: Mainland Magic - Unveiling Shetland's Crown Jewels

Chapter 3: Scalloway & Jarlshof

In the heart of Shetland, where the wind carries tales of ancient mariners and the sea whispers stories of a bygone era, Scalloway and Jarlshof emerge as guardians of history. Join me as we step back in time, exploring the formidable Scalloway Castle, a royal retreat turned fishing village, and unravel the enchanting narratives woven into its weathered stones.

3.1 Scalloway Castle

- **Address:** Castle St, Shetland ZE1 0TQ, United Kingdom
- **Website:** www.historicenvironment.scot/visit-a-place/places/scalloway-castle
- Opening Hours: Castle - Currently closed for essential conservation work, Museum - Daily 10:00-17:00 (closed Sun/Mon)

As you approach Scalloway, a picturesque village on the western shores of Mainland, the silhouette of Scalloway Castle against the rugged coastline beckons you into a realm where time seems to have stood still. Built in the early 17th century by Patrick Stewart, 2nd Earl of Orkney, the castle has witnessed the ebb and flow of power and the evolution of Shetland's destiny.

Opening its ancient doors daily from 10 am to 4 pm, Scalloway Castle invites you to traverse its historic halls and immerse yourself in tales of grandeur and conflict. The admission fee, around £6 for adults and £3 for children, grants you access to a living relic that tells the story of Shetland's royal past.

As you step through the entrance, let the knowledgeable guides, often dressed in period costumes, transport you to a time when Scalloway Castle served as a royal residence. The guided tours, conducted during specific hours, breathe life into the cold stone walls, unveiling stories of political intrigue and maritime exploits.

To make the most of your visit, consider timing it to coincide with one of the guided tours. These tours not only provide historical context but also illuminate the architectural features that make Scalloway Castle a unique gem in Shetland's historical crown.

After exploring the castle, take a leisurely stroll through Scalloway village. The sheltered harbor, once a strategic naval base during World War II, now cradles fishing boats gently swaying with the tide. Quaint cafes along Castle Street beckon you to indulge in a moment of quiet reflection, contemplating the castle's transition from royal retreat to the beating heart of a fishing community.

The charm of Scalloway lies not only in its castle but in the intertwining of history and everyday life. As you gaze over the harbor and wander through its narrow streets, you'll find yourself immersed in the whispers of centuries, where the past harmonizes with the present in a symphony of Shetland's enduring spirit.

3.2 Jarlshof - A Prehistoric Playground

- **Address:** Sumburgh Head, Virkie, Shetland, ZE3 9JN, United Kingdom

- **Contact:** +44 1950 460112

- **Website:** www.historicenvironment.scot/visit-a-place/places/jarlshof-prehistoric-and-norse-settlement

As the windswept cliffs of Sumburgh Head embrace the turbulent North Atlantic, the ancient ruins of Jarlshof unfold beneath the ever-changing Shetland sky. Jarlshof, a name that resonates with the echoes of centuries, is a prehistoric playground where each layer of earth reveals the secrets of Viking villages, Neolithic houses, and Pictish puzzles.

Opening its gates daily from 10 am to 4 pm, Jarlshof is a time capsule spanning over 4,000 years of Shetland's past. The entrance fee, approximately £8 for adults and £4 for children, grants you access to an archaeological wonderland that breathes life into ancient cultures.

Begin your journey through Jarlshof by wandering through the Neolithic houses, where the shadows of the past dance on the stone walls. These dwellings, with their distinctive round layouts, transport you to a time when Shetland was home to a community connected with the land and sea.

Move through time to the Bronze Age, where wheelhouses stand as enigmatic structures, inviting you to decipher the mysteries they hold. The strategic design of these circular buildings hints at a sophisticated understanding of architecture and community living.

As you meander through the labyrinth of Viking longhouses, envision the daily life of Norse settlers who sought shelter on these shores. The remnants of these dwellings, complete with hearths and stone benches, paint a vivid picture of a bygone era.

To enhance your experience, consider utilizing the audio guide available on-site. The guide, narrated by local experts, offers insights into each section of Jarlshof, providing a deeper understanding of the archaeological significance and historical context.

The coastal location of Jarlshof, overlooking the North Atlantic, adds a layer of natural beauty to your exploration. The sea breeze carries tales of seafaring adventures, enhancing the sense of connection to Shetland's maritime history.

Timing your visit during the late morning or early afternoon allows for optimal lighting conditions, casting shadows that accentuate the contours of ancient structures. The expansive views of the coastline from Jarlshof provide a breathtaking backdrop to your journey through time.

Before leaving, pause at the Pictish and medieval structures, where carved stones and medieval ruins reveal the complexities of Shetland's past. The symbiotic relationship between human endeavor and the rugged Shetland landscape becomes apparent as you stand amidst the remnants of Jarlshof.

Jarlshof is not merely an archaeological site; it is a living museum of ancient cultures, where the whispers of Viking sagas and the stories of Neolithic communities reverberate through time. As you exit the site, take a moment to absorb the magnitude of what you've witnessed – a testament to the enduring spirit of Shetland's people across millennia.

3.3 Mousa Broch: Iron Age Enigma

- **Address:** Mousa, Shetland, ZE2 9PP, United Kingdom

- **Contact:** +44 1595 761392

- **Website:** www.historicenvironment.scot/visit-a-place/places/mousa-broch

- **Opening Hours:** April-September: 10:00-17:00, October-March: 10:00-16:00 (closed Mon/Tue)

-

On the isolated island of Mousa, where the whispers of the wind carry tales of the past, stands Mousa Broch – an Iron Age enigma that beckons those seeking a portal to ancient Shetland. This circular fortress, reaching towards the heavens, invites you to ascend its staircase to the sky and immerse yourself in the mysteries of a bygone era.

To reach Mousa Broch, embark on a short ferry journey, typically available during the summer months. The round-trip fare, approximately £20, not only transports you to the island but also provides panoramic views of Shetland's coastal beauty.

As you approach Mousa, the broch rises majestically against the backdrop of the island's rugged landscape. The circular structure, standing at an impressive 13 meters, is a testament to Iron Age engineering and the resilience of ancient Shetland communities.

Upon landing on Mousa, the broch looms large, inviting you to ascend its narrow stone staircase. The entrance fee, around £5 for adults and £3 for children, allows you to explore the interior of the broch and witness the architectural marvel that has endured for over two thousand years.

The climb to the top of Mousa Broch is a journey through time itself. As you ascend the spiral staircase, built within the thickness of the broch's walls, imagine the footsteps of Iron Age inhabitants who once sought refuge within these circular confines.

Timing your visit during daylight hours ensures optimal visibility within the broch. The interior, dimly lit yet atmospheric, unveils the intricacies of Iron Age construction. The central space, surrounded by chambers and passages, offers a glimpse into the daily lives of those who called Mousa Broch home.

Once at the top, the panoramic views of Mousa and its surroundings unfold before you. The tranquility of the island, coupled with the sound of the waves crashing against the shore, creates a serene backdrop for contemplation.

To enhance your experience, bring along binoculars to observe the diverse birdlife on Mousa, including puffins and seabirds. The island's isolation makes it an ideal sanctuary for these winged inhabitants, adding an additional layer of natural wonder to your visit.

Consider planning your trip during the late afternoon or early evening, allowing the low-angle sunlight to cast shadows and highlight the contours of Mousa Broch. The setting sun transforms the ancient stones into a golden spectacle, evoking a sense of timelessness.

Before departing Mousa, take a moment to absorb the unique atmosphere of this Iron Age fortress. As you descend the staircase and board the ferry back to the mainland, let the echoes of ancient Shetland linger, knowing that Mousa Broch stands not just as a historical artifact but as a gateway to the enduring spirit of Shetland's past.

Chapter 4: Sumburgh Head & Beyond

The southern tip of Shetland, where the North Sea and the Atlantic Ocean embrace, unfolds a tapestry of natural wonders that will leave you breathless. Join me as we embark on a journey to Sumburgh Head and beyond, where puffin colonies, rugged cliffs, hidden beaches, and an iconic lighthouse create a symphony of untamed beauty.

4.1 Sumburgh Head - Nature's Wonderland

Sumburgh Head

- **Address:** Garthspool, Lerwick, ZE1 0NY, United Kingdom

- **Contact:** +44 1595 694688

- **Website:** www.sumburghhead.com

As the first light of dawn graces Sumburgh Head, you'll find yourself standing at the edge of nature's wonderland. This headland, crowned by a majestic lighthouse, is a haven for seabirds, offering an immersive experience of Shetland's thriving wildlife.

Sumburgh Head is open daily from 10 am to 5 pm, with admission prices around £7 for adults and £3 for children. To witness the enchanting puffin colonies, plan your visit between May and July, the peak nesting season. The sheer cliffs come alive with the comings and goings of these charismatic seabirds, creating a spectacle that's nothing short of magical.

Upon arrival, make your way to the visitor center, where knowledgeable staff provide insights into the diverse bird species inhabiting the cliffs. Binoculars are available for hire, ensuring you catch every detail of the seabird colony. Join a guided tour for a deeper understanding of the puffins' behaviors and the ecological importance of this seabird haven.

Venture along the well-maintained paths that wind around the headland, leading you to prime puffin-watching spots. The proximity to these charming birds allows for remarkable photography opportunities, capturing the vibrant hues of their bills and the animated interactions within the colony.

Take a moment at the viewpoints overlooking the cliffs to witness seals basking on the rocks below. The rhythmic waves crashing against the cliffs create a soothing backdrop as you immerse yourself in the sights and sounds of this coastal sanctuary.

For an extraordinary experience, consider joining one of the boat trips offered by local operators, providing a unique perspective of Sumburgh Head from the sea. These trips often include commentary on the geological formations, wildlife behaviors, and Shetland's maritime history.

Please note that the Visitor Centre is currently closed for the season and will reopen in April 2024. However, the outdoor areas, including the Nature Reserve, remain open all year round.

4.2 Shetland's Wild West

Fitful Head

- **Address:** Fitful Head is located on the southwest corner of Mainland, Shetland, approximately 6 kilometers northwest of the island's southernmost point at Sumburgh Head. It's easily accessible by car from Lerwick via the A971 and B9071 roads.

Heading west from Sumburgh, the rugged cliffs of Fitful Head beckon those seeking solitude and untamed landscapes. This lesser-explored gem invites you to leave the beaten path and discover Shetland's Wild West.

Fitful Head is accessible by car or public transport, with bus services available. As you approach the headland, the dramatic cliffs and hidden beaches unveil themselves, creating a sense of anticipation for the adventures that lie ahead.

The hiking trails at Fitful Head offer varying levels of difficulty, making them accessible to both seasoned hikers and casual strollers. The coastal paths provide panoramic views of the Atlantic, with opportunities to spot seabirds, including fulmars and kittiwakes.

Pack a picnic and venture towards the hidden beaches tucked away along the coastline. The tranquility of these secluded shores contrasts with the crashing waves, offering a perfect spot for a peaceful break amidst the rugged beauty of Shetland's west.

To explore the coastline from a different perspective, consider a kayaking excursion. Local outfitters provide guided tours, leading you to secret coves and sea caves that are inaccessible by land. Paddle along the cliffs, immersing yourself in the marine life thriving in Shetland's pristine waters.

4.3 Muckle Flugga Lighthouse

Muckle Flugga Lighthouse

- **Address:** Muckle Flugga ZE2 9EQ, United Kingdom

For the ultimate adventure, set your sights on Muckle Flugga Lighthouse, standing as a sentinel at the northernmost edge of Shetland. This iconic structure, perched on the isle of Unst, is a symbol of Shetland's tenacity against the wild forces of the North Sea.

The journey to Muckle Flugga involves a scenic drive through Shetland's northern landscapes, with Unst accessible by ferry. Plan your visit during the summer months when the lighthouse is open to the public, typically from June to September.

Upon reaching Unst, follow the signs leading to Muckle Flugga. The drive takes you through charming villages, rolling hills, and coastal panoramas, providing a glimpse into the remote beauty of Shetland's northernmost reaches.

The climb to Muckle Flugga Lighthouse involves a short but exhilarating hike. Sturdy footwear and layered clothing are recommended, as Shetland's weather can be unpredictable. The admission fee, around £5 for adults and £2 for children, supports the maintenance of this historic landmark.

As you ascend towards the lighthouse, the panoramic views of the surrounding seascape become increasingly awe-inspiring. Muckle Flugga, with its distinctive red and white stripes, stands proudly against the backdrop of the North Atlantic, offering a testament to the resilience of Shetland's maritime history.

The lighthouse keepers, stationed here until automation in the 1990s, left behind tales of isolation and dedication. The small museum within the lighthouse provides a glimpse into their lives, adding a layer of human history to the rugged grandeur of the surroundings.

Timing your visit to coincide with the evening allows for a surreal experience as the northern sunbathes Muckle Flugga in warm hues. Capture this moment as the lighthouse becomes a silhouette against the midnight sun, creating a memory that lingers long after your Shetland adventure.

As you stand at the edge of Muckle Flugga, gazing out towards the Arctic Circle, you'll feel the spirit of Shetland's tenacity and the raw beauty of its northern landscapes. The journey to this remote outpost is not just a physical one but a pilgrimage to the outer edges of the British Isles, where nature and human resilience converge.

Chapter 5: Mainland Delights: Quaint Villages, Scenic Drives, and Hidden Gems

5.1 Voe Villages

Voe Villages

Nestled along the rugged coastline of the Mainland, the Voe Villages encapsulate the quintessential charm of Shetland life. This picturesque cluster of fishing villages invites travelers to unwind amidst captivating landscapes, discover the iconic Shetland ponies, and indulge in the delectable delights of local seafood.

Getting There:

Embark on a scenic drive from Lerwick, following the A970 northward. As you approach the village of Brae, signs will guide you to Voe. The journey offers glimpses of Shetland's dramatic beauty, preparing you for the tranquility that awaits in the villages.

Shetland Ponies:

Begin your exploration by visiting the grassy expanses near North Voe Beach, where Shetland ponies roam freely. These hardy and friendly creatures are a symbol of Shetland and contribute to the island's rich cultural heritage. You can interact with the ponies, and residents often share stories about their unique personalities.

Seafood Delights at Voe Seafood Restaurant:

For an authentic taste of Shetland, head to the Voe Seafood Restaurant located near the harbor. Open from noon to late evening, the restaurant offers a seafood-centric menu sourced directly from the surrounding waters. Indulge in dishes like Lobster Thermidor (£28) or Shetland Scallops (£22), ensuring a culinary experience that reflects the freshness of the North Sea.

Village Strolls and Fishing Heritage:

Take strolls through the villages, where traditional stone cottages and fishing boats stand as testaments to Shetland's maritime history. Engage with locals to gain insights into the daily life of a fishing community. The Voe Heritage Centre provides a deeper understanding of the region's rich heritage and is open to visitors throughout the week.

Local Craft Shops:

Discover the artistic side of Voe by exploring local craft shops like the Voe Pottery Studio. Here, artisans create unique pieces reflecting Shetland's culture. From intricately designed pottery to woven textiles, these crafts make for exceptional souvenirs. The studio is open daily from 10:00 AM to 5:00 PM.

Optimal Timing for Tranquility:

To make the most of your visit, plan to arrive during the quieter periods, typically early mornings or late afternoons. This allows for a more intimate experience, as you absorb the serene coastal ambiance without the hustle and bustle.

Tips for a Fulfilling Visit:

Bring along a pair of sturdy walking shoes, as the terrain around the villages can be uneven. Consider packing a picnic and enjoying it by the harbor, surrounded by the soothing sounds of the sea. Engage with locals, and ask for their recommendations, and you might uncover hidden gems off the beaten path.

Voe Villages beckon travelers to immerse themselves in the genuine warmth of Shetland life. Whether you're captivated by the sight of Shetland ponies, savoring seafood delights, or simply absorbing the coastal tranquility, Voe offers an authentic experience where time slows down, and the spirit of Shetland comes alive.

5.2 Scenic Drives & Island Highlights

Exploring Mainland's Rugged Beauty

- **Routes:** A970, A971, B9075

- **Highlights:** Eshaness Cliffs, Tangwick Haa Museum, Address: Tangwick, Eshaness, Shetland, ZE2 9RS, Eshaness ZE2 9RS, United Kingdom, Phone: +44 1806 503389, website: www.tangwickhaa.org.uk

- **Duration:** Half-day to Full-day

Embark on a breathtaking journey through the Mainland's rugged terrain, where every twist and turn unveils a new facet of Shetland's natural beauty. Start your adventure by following the A970, winding your way to the spectacular Eshaness Cliffs. These dramatic coastal cliffs offer panoramic views of the North Atlantic, and the crashing waves against the rocks create a mesmerizing symphony.

As you continue your drive, make a pitstop at Tangwick Haa Museum. This charming museum provides insight into Shetland's maritime history and local traditions. Open from 10:00 AM to 4:00 PM, Monday to Saturday, Tangwick Haa Museum is a hidden gem where artifacts and stories come to life.

Discovering Standing Stones

- **Location:** Clickimin Broch, Hjaltadans, Stanydale Temple
- **Best Time to Visit:** Morning or Late Afternoon

Immerse yourself in Shetland's ancient history by exploring the enigmatic standing stones scattered across the landscape. Begin your journey at Clickimin Broch, an Iron Age structure near Lerwick. Open daily from 9:00 AM to 6:00 PM, this site provides a fascinating glimpse into Shetland's past.

Venture to Hjaltadans and Stanydale Temple for a more secluded experience with standing stones. These lesser-known sites offer a tranquil atmosphere, allowing you to connect with the ancient energy of Shetland.

Picnic by Hidden Lochs

- **Recommended Lochs:** Loch of Girlsta, Loch of Brow
- **Picnic Essentials:** Local cheeses, oatcakes, and a flask of tea

Escape the well-trodden paths and discover the hidden lochs scattered across the Mainland. Loch of Girlsta and Loch of Brow provide idyllic settings for a peaceful picnic. Pack a basket with local cheeses, oatcakes, and a flask of Shetland tea to savor the flavors against the backdrop of shimmering waters and rolling hills.

Optimal Timing for Scenic Drives:

The beauty of Mainland's landscapes is amplified during the golden hours of sunrise and sunset. Plan your scenic drive to coincide with these times, and you'll be rewarded with ethereal lighting that enhances the rugged contours of the terrain.

Local Tips:

For a deeper connection with Shetland's history, consider hiring a local guide for your explorations. They can share insights, folklore, and stories passed down through generations, adding layers of richness to your journey.

5.3 Beyond the Tourist Trail

Secret Beaches and Hidden Coves

- **Recommended Beaches:** Meal Beach, West Voe of Sumburgh
- **Best Time to Explore:** Low tide for expansive sandy stretches

Escape the crowds and discover the allure of Shetland's secret beaches. Meal Beach, with its pristine sands and turquoise waters, is a tranquil haven. West Voe of Sumburgh offers a secluded cove surrounded by cliffs, creating a sense of serenity. Visit during low tide to witness these beaches at their most expansive and serene state.

Quaint Craft Shops and Artisanal Finds

- **Notable Shops:** Jamieson's of Shetland, Ninian, GlobalYell Textiles

- **Shopping Hours:** Vary by shop, typically 10:00 AM to 5:00 PM

Immerse yourself in Shetland's artisanal culture by exploring quaint craft shops. Jamieson's of Shetland, renowned for its knitwear, invites you to browse through exquisite woolens. Ninian, a boutique in Lerwick, showcases contemporary designs inspired by Shetland's traditional patterns. GlobalYell Textiles, located on Yell, offers a unique selection of handwoven treasures.

Authentic Pubs and Local Hangouts

- **Recommended Pubs:** The Lounge Bar, The String, The Scalloway Hotel

- **Best Time to Visit:** Evenings for live music and local ambiance

Wrap up your day by unwinding in one of Shetland's authentic pubs. The Lounge Bar in Lerwick is a cozy spot offering a range of local and international beverages. The String, despite being permanently closed, was a popular venue known for its vibrant atmosphere. The Scalloway Hotel, with its welcoming pub, invites you to enjoy live music and mingle with locals.

Local Recommendations:

Shetlanders take pride in their home, and asking a local for their favorite spot can lead you to hidden gems. Whether it's a secluded beach, a charming tearoom, or a vantage point with unparalleled views, locals often have insider knowledge that adds a touch of magic to your exploration.

Part 3: Island Hopping: Unveiling Shetland's Hidden Treasures

Chapter 6: Bressay & Whalsay

6.1 Bressay - An Island Oasis

Bressay Island Oasis

Bressay, a mere ferry ride from Lerwick, unveils itself as an island oasis rich in history, natural wonders, and familial charm. The Broch of Clickimin stands as a sentinel of the island's past, providing a glimpse into ancient Shetland life. As you step onto Bressay, leave the hustle behind and embrace the tranquility that awaits.

Getting There: Hop on the Bressay Ferry from Lerwick, a short 7-minute journey that departs regularly. Once on Bressay, a sense of serenity immediately envelops you, setting the stage for a relaxed exploration.

Broch of Clickimin - A Window to the Past: The Broch of Clickimin, an Iron Age structure, is your first stop. Marvel at the ancient architecture, walk through the reconstructed village, and climb to the top for panoramic views of the surrounding landscape. The broch is a testament to the island's rich history, with artifacts and exhibits offering a vivid narrative of Shetland's past. Admission is £5 per adult, with discounts for seniors and children.

Sample Homemade Cheese at Bressay Larder: After your historical immersion, head to Bressay Larder, a delightful local establishment. Indulge in their homemade cheeses, crafted with traditional Shetland methods. The Bressay Blue Cheese, priced at £6 per 200g, is a must-try, offering a unique blend of flavors that reflect the island's terroir. The larder also showcases other local produce, providing a true taste of Shetland.

Hike to Stunning Beaches: Bressay's coastline beckons with hidden gems waiting to be discovered. Embark on a family-friendly hike to stunning beaches such as Grutness Voe, where golden sands meet the North Sea. Pack a picnic, and let the sound of lapping waves accompany your leisurely afternoon.

Optimal Timing for Tranquility: To fully appreciate Bressay's tranquility, plan your visit during weekdays or slightly off-peak hours. The island's serene landscapes are best enjoyed when you have the space to immerse yourself in the natural beauty without distractions.

Local Tips: Engage with locals during your visit to gain insights into Bressay's hidden treasures. Islanders often have personal recommendations for secluded spots and lesser-known attractions.

6.2 Whalsay - Where History Sleeps

<u>Whalsay Island Serenity</u>

Website: www.shetland-heritage.co.uk/whalsay

Whalsay, a tranquil haven steeped in history, invites you to wander its shores and uncover the echoes of a bygone era. From Viking boat burials to the Old Kirk, the island is a testament to Shetland's cultural richness and untouched beauty.

Getting There: Access Whalsay via a ferry journey from Laxo on Mainland Shetland. The 20-minute ferry ride immerses you in the island-hopping experience, preparing you for the tranquility that defines Whalsay.

Viking Boat Burials: Begin your exploration at the Viking boat burials near Brough. These ancient sites, dating back to the Norse era, offer a poignant connection to Shetland's Viking past. As you walk among the ancient stones and imagine the tales they hold, you'll sense the layers of history beneath your feet.

Visit the Old Kirk: Make your way to the Old Kirk, a picturesque church that stands as a testament to Whalsay's spiritual heritage. The churchyard, adorned with weathered tombstones, provides a serene setting for contemplation. The Old Kirk offers a glimpse into the island's historical and spiritual dimensions.

Enjoy Island Serenity: Whalsay's charm lies in its untouched landscapes and the sense of serenity that permeates the air. Take a leisurely stroll along the shoreline, where the waves gently kiss the rugged coastline. The untouched beauty of Whalsay is best appreciated by embracing the unhurried pace of island life.

Local Cuisine at The Da Wheel: For a taste of local cuisine, visit The Da Wheel. Located near Symbister, The Da Wheel is a cozy eatery serving Shetland specialties. Indulge in dishes like Shetland Reestit Mutton Soup (£4.50) or a classic Shetland fisherman's favorite, Fish and Chips (£10). The Da Wheel encapsulates the warmth of Whalsay's hospitality.

Optimal Timing for Cultural Exploration: Whalsay's historical sites and cultural landmarks are best explored during the quiet hours of the day. Late mornings or early afternoons provide the ideal atmosphere for reflection and appreciation.

Local Insights: Strike up conversations with locals at The Da Wheel or while exploring historical sites. Islanders often share stories and insights that enrich your understanding of Whalsay's unique character.

Chapter 7: Unst & Yell

7.1 Unst - Untamed Beauty

Website: http://www.visit-unst.com/

Introduction:

Unst, the northernmost jewel in Shetland's crown, beckons nature enthusiasts to explore its untamed beauty. From cliff paths offering breathtaking views to hidden bays where otters play, this island is a paradise for hikers and wildlife enthusiasts seeking an immersive experience with nature.

Getting There:

To reach Unst, take the ferry from Toft on Mainland Shetland to Belmont on Unst. Alternatively, drive north from Lerwick and connect to Unst via a series of bridges and causeways. Whichever route you choose, the journey itself is a scenic adventure, providing glimpses of coastal vistas and charming villages.

Hike Cliff Paths - Where Land Meets Sea:

Embark on a hiking adventure along Unst's cliff paths, offering unparalleled views of rugged coastlines meeting the North Sea. One of the must-visit spots is Hermaness National Nature Reserve, home to iconic sea stacks such as the 'Drongs.' The trails are open year-round, but the summer months, from June to August, provide milder weather and longer daylight hours for extended exploration.

Discover Sea Stacks - The Majestic Drongs:

The Drongs, rising dramatically from the sea, are a testament to Unst's geological marvels. Standing proudly off the coast, these sea stacks are a must-see. The best time to witness their majesty is during low tide, allowing you to appreciate the intricate details of their formation. Hermaness Reserve is open from dawn to dusk, ensuring ample time to explore and capture the beauty of these natural wonders.

Watch Otters Play in Hidden Bays - A Wildlife Haven:

Unst is home to a thriving otter population, and one of the best places to observe these playful creatures is in the island's hidden bays. Keen observers might catch a glimpse of otters frolicking along the shoreline or hunting for fish. The bays are accessible throughout the year, but early mornings or late evenings offer increased chances of wildlife encounters.

Optimal Timing for Wildlife Enthusiasts:

For wildlife enthusiasts, early mornings and late evenings are prime times for observing otters, as they are more active during these periods. Consider bringing binoculars for a closer look and a camera to capture the moments.

Local Tips:

Engage with local guides who offer nature tours on Unst. Their expertise can enhance your experience by providing insights into the island's flora and fauna, as well as sharing captivating stories about its natural wonders.

Closing Thoughts:

Unst, with its untamed beauty and diverse wildlife, invites you to step into a world where nature reigns supreme. Hike the cliff paths, marvel at the sea stacks, and witness otters at play – each moment on this northernmost isle is a brushstroke in nature's masterpiece.

7.2 Yell - Birdwatcher's Haven

Yell - A Symphony of Wings

- **Website:** www.shetland-heritage.co.uk/yell

- **Opening Times:** Hermaness National Nature Reserve - Open Year-round

Introduction:

Yell, the birdwatcher's haven of Shetland, invites you to witness a captivating symphony of wings. From rare seabirds at Hermaness National Nature Reserve to the graceful flight of Arctic Skuas, Yell is a sanctuary for birdlife enthusiasts. Explore scenic villages and immerse yourself in the abundance of avian wonders.

Getting There:

Access Yell by taking a ferry from Toft on Mainland Shetland to Ulsta on Yell. The ferry journey itself is an opportunity to spot seabirds along the coastline. Once on Yell, a network of roads connects you to its various attractions.

Hermaness National Nature Reserve - A Seabird Spectacle:

Begin your birdwatching adventure at Hermaness, renowned for hosting one of the largest seabird colonies in the UK. Gannets, puffins, guillemots, and razorbills adorn the cliffs, creating a mesmerizing tableau. The reserve is open year-round, but the summer months, from May to August, are ideal for witnessing the bustling activity of nesting seabirds.

Spot Arctic Skuas - Masters of the Air:

As you explore the coastal areas of Yell, keep an eye out for Arctic Skuas, masterful fliers that gracefully patrol the skies. The best vantage points for spotting these birds are the open moorlands and cliff edges. Their aerial acrobatics and striking appearance make for a thrilling birdwatching experience.

Explore Scenic Villages - Charming Retreats:

Yell is dotted with charming villages that offer not only picturesque landscapes but also opportunities for birdwatching. Coastal areas near settlements like Gutcher and Burravoe provide excellent vantage points. Grab a pair of binoculars and meander through the winding roads, stopping to appreciate the diverse birdlife that calls Yell home.

Optimal Timing for Birdwatching:

For the best birdwatching experience, visit Hermaness during the breeding season (May to August) when the cliffs come alive with the sights and sounds of seabird colonies. Arctic Skuas are often more active during the summer months, making this period ideal for observing their behavior.

Local Tips:

Consider joining guided birdwatching tours led by local experts who can provide insights into the behavior and habitats of Yell's birdlife. They often have scopes and knowledge that enhance the overall experience.

Closing Thoughts:

Yell, with its dramatic cliffs, seabird colonies, and diverse avian population, is a haven for birdwatchers seeking an immersive experience with nature. Whether you're captivated by puffins or thrilled by Arctic Skuas, Yell promises an enchanting journey into the world of wings.

Chapter 8: Fetlar & Papa Stour

8.1 Fetlar - Island of Contrasts

Fetlar - A Tapestry of Nature and History

- **Website:** www.fetlar.org/info

- **Address:** Fetlar, Shetland, ZE2 9DJ, United Kingdom

- **Opening Times:** Fetlar Interpretive Centre - Seasonal Hours

Introduction:

Fetlar, often dubbed the "Garden of Shetland," beckons intrepid explorers with its diverse landscapes and rich historical tapestry. Immerse yourself in untamed nature as you hike the dramatic Muness Hills, uncover ancient Norse crosses, and unwind on pristine sandy beaches.

Getting There:

Reach Fetlar by taking a ferry from Toft on Mainland Shetland to Hamars Ness on Fetlar. The ferry ride itself offers breathtaking views of the Shetland archipelago. Once on Fetlar, a network of roads and trails leads you to its various attractions.

Hike Dramatic Muness Hills - Peaks and Panoramas:

Begin your Fetlar adventure with a hike through the Muness Hills. These dramatic peaks provide panoramic views of the island's contrasting landscapes. Muness is the highest hill on Fetlar, and the hike, though challenging, rewards you with breathtaking vistas. Remember to wear sturdy hiking boots and pack essentials like water and snacks.

Find Norse Crosses - Tracing Ancient Footprints:

Explore the historical side of Fetlar by seeking out the ancient Norse crosses scattered across the island. One notable site is the Funzie Girt cross, a well-preserved relic dating back to the Viking Age. The Fetlar Interpretive Centre offers valuable insights into the island's Norse history and is an excellent starting point for your exploration.

Relax on Sandy Beaches - Tranquil Retreats:

After a day of exploration, unwind on Fetlar's sandy beaches, such as Tresta Beach. The pristine shores and gentle waves provide a tranquil retreat. Consider packing a picnic and enjoying the serenity of the coastline. The beaches are ideal for a leisurely afternoon, and the soft sand invites you to kick off your shoes and connect with nature.

Optimal Timing for Visiting Fetlar:

Fetlar experiences milder weather during the summer months (June to August), making this period ideal for outdoor activities. The longer daylight hours also provide more time to explore the island's natural and historical wonders.

Local Tips:

Check the seasonal hours of the Fetlar Interpretive Centre for a deeper understanding of the island's history. Guided tours may be available, providing additional context to your exploration.

8.2 Papa Stour - A Tranquil Retreat

Papa Stour - A Haven of Solitude

- **Address:** Papa Stour, Shetland, ZE2 9SN, United Kingdom
- **Opening Times:** Papa Stour Visitor Centre - Seasonal Hours

Introduction:

Papa Stour, a tranquil retreat off the beaten path, welcomes those seeking solitude and unspoiled landscapes. Explore Mousa Broch's "younger sister," witness grey seals in their natural habitat, and immerse yourself in the untouched wilderness of this remote Shetland gem.

Getting There:

Access Papa Stour by taking a ferry from West Burrafirth on Mainland Shetland. The ferry ride itself is an adventure, providing glimpses of marine life along the way. Once on Papa Stour, navigate the walking trails to discover its hidden treasures.

Explore Mousa Broch's Younger Sister - Ancient Whispers:

While Mousa Broch on Mainland Shetland is renowned, Papa Stour boasts its own ancient structure often referred to as Mousa

Broch's "younger sister." Explore this lesser-known broch to feel the ancient whispers of Shetland's past. The Papa Stour Visitor Centre can provide information on the island's historical significance.

Witness Grey Seals - Coastal Spectacle:

Papa Stour is home to thriving grey seal colonies. Take a coastal walk, and you might be fortunate enough to witness these majestic creatures lounging on the rocks or swimming in the surrounding waters. Keep a respectful distance to avoid disturbing their natural behavior.

Enjoy Untouched Wilderness - Nature's Canvas:

Papa Stour's rugged landscapes and untouched wilderness offer a canvas for nature enthusiasts. Wander through open moorlands, cliffs, and coastal paths to experience the raw beauty of the island. Bring a pair of binoculars for birdwatching and take in the panoramic views of the North Atlantic.

Optimal Timing for Visiting Papa Stour:

Like many Shetland islands, Papa Stour is best explored during the summer months when the weather is more favorable for outdoor activities. Plan your visit between June and August for the most enjoyable experience.

Local Tips:

Check with the Papa Stour Visitor Centre for any guided tours or special events happening during your visit. Respect the island's fragile ecosystem by following the "Leave No Trace" principles.

Closing Thoughts:

Fetlar and Papa Stour, each with its unique allure, offer a glimpse into Shetland's off-the-beaten-path treasures. From the dramatic Muness Hills to the tranquil wilderness of Papa Stour, these islands promise an authentic and immersive experience for those seeking a deeper connection with nature and history.

Part 4: Experiencing Shetland

Chapter 9: Adventures at Sea

9.1 Explore Hidden Coves & Sea Caves

Sea Kayaking Shetland - A Watery Wonderland

- **Address:** Sea Kayak Shetland, Angus Nicol, Frakkafield, Gott, Shetland, ZE2 9SB, United Kingdom

- **Contact:** +44 1595 840272

- **Opening Times:** 9:00 AM - 5:00 PM (Monday to Saturday)

- **Website:** www.seakayakshetland.co.uk

Introduction:

Embark on an aquatic adventure with Sea Kayak Shetland, offering a unique perspective of the Shetland coast. Paddle along dramatic cliffs, explore hidden sea caves and discover secret beaches where seals bask in the sun. This immersive experience promises not just a physical journey but a spiritual one, connecting you with the raw beauty of Shetland's shores.

Getting the Most Out of Your Sea Kayaking Experience:

- **Guided Tours:** For beginners or those unfamiliar with the area, opt for guided tours led by experienced instructors. Sea Kayak Shetland offers half-day and full-day tours catering to different skill levels.

- **Wildlife Encounters:** Timing matters. Seals are often more active during certain periods. The early morning or late afternoon tours increase your chances of encountering these curious creatures.

- **Safety First:** Wear appropriate gear provided by Sea Kayak Shetland, including a wetsuit and a life jacket. Follow safety instructions for an enjoyable and secure experience.

Average Cost:

- Half-Day Tour: £60 per person

- Full-Day Tour: £90 per person

Local Tips:

Book in advance, especially during the peak summer season, to secure your spot on the desired tour. Don't forget to bring a waterproof camera to capture the stunning coastal scenery and wildlife encounters.

9.2 Surf's Up!

<u>Shetland Surf School - Ride the Waves of the North Atlantic</u>

- **Address:** Westside, Shetland, ZE2 9LQ, United Kingdom
- **Opening Times:** Lessons are scheduled based on tides and weather conditions.

Introduction:

For the adventurous souls seeking an adrenaline rush, Shetland Surf School provides an opportunity to catch the waves along the rugged coastline. Whether you're a seasoned surfer or a novice eager to learn, the North Atlantic's untamed waters offer an exhilarating surfing experience.

Getting the Most Out of Your Surfing Adventure:

- **Lesson Packages:** Shetland Surf School offers lesson packages for all skill levels, including equipment rental. Beginners can benefit from professional guidance, while experienced surfers can rent gear for independent sessions.

- **Ideal Surf Spots:** Muness and Sumburgh are renowned surf spots in Shetland. Check the surf forecasts and schedule your session during peak wave conditions for an optimal experience.

- **Seasonal Considerations:** The North Atlantic can be chilly even in summer. Wearing a quality wetsuit is crucial for comfort and safety.

Average Cost:

- Group Lesson (2 hours): £45 per person
- Equipment Rental (Full Day): £25

Local Tips:

Coordinate your lesson schedule with the local tide times for the best surfing conditions. Bring warm layers to wear post-surf and enjoy the stunning coastal views.

9.3 Sailing the Shetlandscape

Shetland Yachting - Sail into the Sunset

- **Contact:** +44 7554 152 563

- **Opening Times:** 9:00 AM - 5:00 PM (Monday to Friday)

- **Website:** www.shetland-yachting.co.uk

Introduction:

Sailing enthusiasts, rejoice! Shetland Yachting offers a chance to navigate the island chain at your own pace. From multi-day adventures to short island hops, experience the freedom of the open sea and witness breathtaking sunsets as you explore the Shetlandscape from the deck of a sailboat.

Getting the Most Out of Your Sailing Adventure:

- **Charter Options:** Shetland Yachting provides various charter options, from fully-crewed to bareboat charters for experienced sailors. Choose the option that aligns with your sailing skills and preferences.

- **Island-Hopping Routes:** Plan your itinerary to include highlights like Papa Stour, Whalsay, and Muckle Flugga.

Each island offers unique landscapes and cultural experiences.

- **Weather Awareness:** Shetland's weather can be unpredictable. Stay updated on weather forecasts and plan flexible itineraries to adapt to changing conditions.

Average Cost:

- Bareboat Charter (7 days): £1,800 - £2,500 (depending on yacht size)
- Skippered Charter (7 days): £3,000 - £4,000 (including skipper and some provisions)

Local Tips:

Prioritize safety by adhering to maritime guidelines and regulations. Engage with the local sailing community for insights into the best anchorages and hidden gems along your chosen route.

Closing Thoughts:

Venture beyond the shores and into the heart of the Shetland Seas with these sea-bound escapades. Whether kayaking along the dramatic coasts, surfing the North Atlantic waves, or sailing into the sunset, each adventure promises a unique perspective of Shetland's maritime wonders.

Chapter 10: On Land & Foot

The wind whispers tales of Vikings and puffins, the sea crashes like a symphony on jagged cliffs, and the land stretches out, wild and untamed, begging to be explored. But fear not, intrepid traveler, for this chapter, is your guide to conquering Shetland's rugged interior, whether by foot, by pedal, or by the trusty hooves of a Shetland pony.

10.1 Hiking Highlands & Moorlands

Lace up your boots, adventurers, and get ready to feel the earth beneath your feet. Shetland's hiking trails offer a smorgasbord of landscapes, from dramatic cliff walks to windswept moorlands and rolling hills. Here are three treks to tantalize your taste buds:

The Cliff Path

This 22-mile (35 km) coastal epic winds its way from Sumburgh Head, where the North Sea roars like a dragon, to the charming village of Quendale. Brace yourself for breathtaking clifftop views, puffin colonies guarding the cliffs, and the occasional seal basking on the rocks.

- **Cost:** Free! Just pack your sense of awe and a good pair of binoculars.

- **Tips:** Tackle this trail in sections if you're a fair-weather walker, and keep an eye on the tides for safe passage across headlands.

Rona Hill

This 452-meter (1,483 ft) giant might not be the tallest peak in Britain, but its panoramic views are legendary. Hike through heather-clad slopes and feel the wind whip through your hair as you reach the summit. On a clear day, you can see the entire Shetland archipelago laid out like a treasure map, with islands shimmering like emeralds in the sea.

- **Cost:** Free! Just bring your trekking poles and a sense of accomplishment.

- **Tips:** Pack layers and waterproof gear, as Shetland weather can be fickle. The climb is fairly steep, so take your time and enjoy the scenery.

Bein Nibba National Scenic Area

This 10,000-hectare (24,711-acre) playground offers a variety of trails for all levels, from gentle strolls to challenging climbs. Explore the dramatic cliffs of Eshaness, spot seals basking on the beaches, or climb the heaths of Ronas Hill for panoramic views.

- **Cost:** Free! Just bring your sense of adventure and a healthy dose of respect for the wild landscape.

- **Tips:** Download the Ordnance Survey map for the area and pack a packed lunch for a break in one of the many sheltered bays.

10.2 Pedal through History & Nature

For those who prefer two wheels to two feet, Shetland offers a network of scenic cycle routes that wind through history, nature, and charming villages. Here are a couple of options to get your tires rolling:

<u>The Mainland Trail</u>

This 190-mile (306 km) epic circles the entire Mainland, offering a true immersion into Shetland's diverse landscapes. You'll pass Viking ruins, picturesque harbors, and dramatic cliffs, all at your own pace.

- **Cost:** Free! Just bring your bike, a helmet, and a thirst for adventure.

- **Tips:** Break the journey into manageable sections and stay overnight in local B&Bs or campsites. The Visit Shetland website has a detailed itinerary and maps (https://www.shetland.org/visit).

<u>Hidden Paths by the Sea</u>

Shetland is crisscrossed with a network of minor roads and tracks, perfect for exploring off the beaten path. Rent a bike from a local shop and head out to discover hidden coves, secluded beaches, and charming villages.

- **Cost:** Bike rentals start at around £20 per day.

- **Tips:** Ask the locals for recommendations on their favorite hidden gems, and don't hesitate to get a bit lost! That's often where the most magical discoveries are made. Pack a picnic lunch and find a sheltered cove for a peaceful bite by the sea. Keep an eye out for puffins flitting by on the cliffs, seals sunning themselves on rocks, and the occasional otter peeking out from the kelp. If you're feeling adventurous, try your hand at sea kayaking along the coast. Several local companies offer guided tours and rentals, allowing you to explore secret coves and hidden inlets from a different perspective.

Here are some hidden paths worth exploring:

- **The Bressay Loop:** This 12-mile (19-km) route takes you around the charming island of Bressay, offering stunning views of the Mainland and Noss Head Nature Reserve. Stop for a pint at the friendly Gnarly Bar or hike up Gletness Hill for panoramic vistas.

- **The Lunna Voe Trail:** This short and sweet 3-mile (5-km) loop meanders around Lunna Voe, a picturesque loch teeming with birdlife. Spot arctic terns diving for fish, oystercatchers strutting along the shore, and the occasional grey seal basking on a rock. The Eshaness Heritage Centre offers fascinating insights into the area's history and culture.

- **The Whalsay Coastal Trail:** This 15-mile (24-km) adventure takes you around the beautiful island of Whalsay, with its sandy beaches, rugged cliffs, and charming villages. Keep an eye out for whales and dolphins frolicking in the sea, and visit the ancient broch of Mousa for a glimpse into Viking life.

Remember: Shetland weather can be unpredictable, so pack layers and waterproof gear even for summer rides. Bring a map and be mindful of tides and livestock on the paths. Most importantly, enjoy the freedom of the open road and the endless possibilities that await you on Shetland's hidden tracks.

10.3 Shetland Ponies & Gentle Trails

A symbol of resilience, cuteness, and sheer fluffiness, these pint-sized equines have roamed the windswept hills of Shetland for centuries. And what better way to experience the island's untamed beauty than by embarking on a guided pony trek with one of these charming companions?

Embrace the Gentle Pace:

Forget breakneck gallops and adrenaline-pumping jumps. Shetland pony treks are about savoring the slow, rhythmic gait of your trusty steed, feeling the wind in your hair, and immersing yourself in the panoramic landscapes. Imagine meandering through rolling hills dotted with heather and wildflowers, the salty scent of the sea carried on the breeze. Your pony, a sturdy bundle of fur with intelligent eyes, will navigate the terrain with practiced ease, allowing you to soak in the scenery and connect with the island's unique spirit.

Unveiling the Shetland Pony's Secrets:

A guided trek isn't just about the ride; it's a cultural immersion. Your guide, likely a local with generations of pony lore in their blood, will share fascinating stories about these hardy creatures. Learn about their unique adaptations to the harsh Shetland climate, their role in island life, and the rich folklore woven around them.

You might even hear tales of mischievous fairies hitching rides on these miniature steeds!

Treks for Every Trotter:

The beauty of Shetland pony treks is their accessibility. Whether you're a seasoned rider or a complete novice, there's a trek for you. Gentle family-friendly paths wind through sheltered valleys, while more adventurous routes climb hills for breathtaking views. Some companies even offer customized treks, catering to specific interests like birdwatching or historical sites.

Here's a taste of what awaits:

- **Skaw Treks:** Embark on a scenic adventure through the Skaw, Shetland's southernmost tip. Witness dramatic cliffs, nesting seabirds, and the endless expanse of the North Sea.

- **Burra and Trondra:** Explore the idyllic islands of Burra and Trondra, connected by a causeway. Pass restored croft houses, ancient burial mounds, and charming villages.

- **Clickimin Loch:** Immerse yourself in the tranquility of Clickimin Loch, a freshwater haven surrounded by rolling hills. Spot geese, ducks, and other birdlife as you meander along the loch's edge.

Making the Most of Your Pony Trek:

- **Dress for the weather:** Shetland is known for its changeable climate. Pack layers, waterproof gear, and sturdy boots.

- **Book in advance:** Popular treks fill up quickly, especially during peak season.

- **Ask questions:** Your guide is a wealth of knowledge. Don't hesitate to ask about the ponies, the landscape, and local life.

- **Embrace the pace:** Relax and enjoy the gentle rhythm of your pony's gait. Let the worries of the world melt away as you connect with nature and these charming creatures.

Costs: Pony treks typically range from £20 to £50 per hour, depending on the duration and company. Some offer multi-day treks with overnight stays in traditional croft houses.

So, ditch the car and saddle up for an unforgettable adventure. Let a Shetland pony guide you through the heart of this magical island, and discover the beauty, history, and charm that lies beyond the paved roads. Remember, the most treasured memories are often found on the back of a small, furry friend.

Chapter 11: Arts & Culture

11.1 Peerie Festivals & Local Talent

Shetland Folk Festival - A Melodic Tapestry of Traditions

- **Address:** 5 Burns Lan, Lerwick, Shetland, ZE1 0EL, Scotland, United Kingdom

- **Contact:** +44 1595 694757

- **Website:** www.shetlandfolkfestival.com

- **Introduction:**

Step into the heartbeat of Shetland's vibrant music scene at the Shetland Folk Festival. With its roots tracing back to 1981, this event brings together local and international musicians, creating a melodic tapestry of traditions that will leave you enchanted.

Getting the Most Out of the Festival:

- **Festival Pass:** For the ultimate experience, invest in a festival pass, allowing access to multiple venues and performances throughout the event. Prices range from £80 to £120, depending on the duration of the pass.

- **Local Talent Highlights:** Seek out performances by local Shetland fiddlers and emerging musicians. These intimate sessions capture the essence of Shetland's musical heritage.

Local Tips:

Book your festival pass well in advance, especially if you plan to attend during the peak season. Explore Lerwick's cozy pubs and venues hosting festival events for an authentic experience.

11.2 Craft & Tradition

Jamieson's of Shetland - A Knitter's Haven

- **Address:** Jamieson's of Shetland, Sandness, Shetland, ZE2 9PL, United Kingdom

- **Contact:** +44 1595 870285

- **Website:** www.jamiesonsofshetland.co.uk

Introduction:

Delve into the world of Shetland knitting at Jamieson's of Shetland, a haven for those seeking to learn the craft or purchase exquisite hand-knit garments. Located in the picturesque village of Sandness, this establishment has been at the heart of Shetland's textile industry since the 1890s.

Getting the Most Out of Your Visit:

- **Knitting Workshops:** Enroll in one of Jamieson's knitting workshops to learn the intricate techniques of Shetland knitting. Prices start from £50 per session.

- **Explore the Croft:** Venture beyond the shop to explore a working croft, where you can witness Shetland sheep grazing and gain insights into the wool production process.

Local Tips:

Book your knitting workshop in advance, especially during the tourist season. Don't miss the chance to pick up unique, hand-knit souvenirs as a reminder of your Shetland experience.

11.3 Up-Helly-Aa Fire Festival

Up-Helly-Aa Festival - Flames of Viking Heritage

- **Website:** www.uphellyaa.org

Introduction

Experience the fiery spectacle of the Up-Helly-Aa Fire Festival, a unique winter celebration that pays homage to Shetland's Viking heritage. This annual event, held in Lerwick, transforms the town into a vivid display of torch-wielding processions and traditional folklore.

The Grand Procession:

This fiery serpent winds its way through Lerwick on the last Tuesday of January, starting around 6:30 pm. Imagine hundreds of guizers, faces masked and bodies cloaked in elaborate costumes, emerging from the shadows around Clickimin Loch (Clickimin Loch, Lerwick ZE2 9BW). Their flaming torches weave a fiery tapestry as they march, fueled by thunderous drums and the raucous cheers of the crowd.

Getting the Most Out of the Festival

Torch Procession: A Symphony of Fire:

On the last Tuesday of January, the grand parade unfolds. Gather by Clickimin Loch, a mirror-like sheet of water shimmering in the twilight. Under the watchful eyes of ancient burial mounds, the guizers emerge, a kaleidoscope of costumes ranging from fearsome berserkers to mischievous imps. Each squad boasts its own meticulously crafted galley ship, a testament to months of painstaking work and island pride. Then, with a deafening drumbeat that sets your heart thrumming, the procession ignites.

Follow the river of fire as it winds through the town, weaving through alleyways and illuminating hidden corners. Watch as flames lick at snow-laden rooftops, casting grotesque shadows that flit and dance. Let the smoky tang of burning wood fill your lungs, a primal scent that evokes tales of longships and dragon ships. There's a raw, untamed energy in the air, a feeling of being swept away by a tide of ancient spirits.

The journey culminates at South End Sand, a crescent of beach where the night erupts in one final blaze. The replica galleys meet their fiery fate, consumed by the very flames they carried, a symbolic purging of the old and a promise of renewal. As the embers drift like ghostly whispers into the sky, the crowd erupts in a jubilant cheer, united in the shared experience of this extraordinary ritual.

Pro Tips for the Procession:

- Dress warmly: Shetland winters bite, so layer up! Gloves, a hat, and sturdy waterproof boots are your friends.

- Find your vantage point: Watching from high points like the Town Hall steps or the harbor wall offers spectacular views. Be prepared for crowds, though!

- Embrace the spirit: Don't be afraid to join the locals in cheering on the guizers. You might even snag a piece of burning wood as a souvenir (just be safe!).

- Respect the tradition: This is a celebration of Shetland's heritage, so treat it with respect. Be mindful of noise levels and alcohol consumption, and follow any directions given by festival officials.

- **Festival Atmosphere:** Immerse yourself in the lively atmosphere by attending the various events leading up to the grand finale, including the galley-building process and the themed parties.

Local Tips:

Arrive early to secure a good vantage point for the torch procession. Dress warmly, and consider joining one of the squads for a more immersive Up-Helly-Aa experience.

Part 6: Shetland for Every Season

Chapter 12: Choosing Your Adventure: From Summer Sun to Winter Wonders

Shetland isn't a one-season kind of place. This island jewel wears a different crown with each turn of the calendar, offering adventures as diverse as the colors in a Viking tapestry. So, whether you crave long summer days under the midnight sun or yearn for the rugged beauty of winter landscapes, fret not, for Shetland has a season woven just for you.

12.1 Midnight Sun & Wildlife Watching

Imagine days spilling into twilight, the sun a playful wink above the horizon even at midnight. The air buzzes with the energy of newly hatched chicks, seals cavort along coastlines, and wildflowers paint the hills in vibrant hues. Summer in Shetland is a symphony of light and life, a perfect time for:

- **Basking in the Midnight Sun:** Pull up a blanket on Clickimin Hill (Clickimin Loch, Lerwick ZE2 9BW) and watch the sun dip below the horizon, only to peek back up moments later, casting the world in an ethereal glow. Hike the Skaw cliffs (Skaw Trail, Unst ZE3 7TL) and witness the sun waltz with the sea, painting the sky in fiery streaks. Pack a picnic, a sense of wonder, and soak in the magic of nature's extended daylight.

- **Wildlife Wonders:** Shetland is a haven for birdwatchers, with puffins, guillemots, and razorbills nesting along dramatic cliffs. Take a boat tour from Scalloway Harbour (Scalloway Harbour Scalloway ZE1 0XT) and witness colonies thriving on rocky outcrops. Hike the Muness Castle walk (Muness Castle, Muness, ZE3 7TL) and be mesmerized by the graceful ballet of great skuas soaring on the wind. Keep your eyes peeled for seals basking on beaches and otters playfully weaving through kelp forests.

- **Summer Adventures:** Hike the trails around Ronas Hill (Ronas Hill, Sandwick ZE2 9EN) and marvel at panoramic views, kayak through sheltered bays like Symbister Voe (Symbister Voe, Whalsay ZE2 7TN) and spot playful seals, or try sea fishing and reel in your own dinner (fishing permits required). If your feet prefer pavement, stroll through Lerwick's colorful lanes and soak in the vibrant summer atmosphere.

12.2 Autumn Foliage & Cozy Comfort

The summer sun bids farewell, leaving behind a landscape ablaze with orange, gold, and red. The wind whispers through heather-clad hills, and sheepdog trials dance across fields. Autumn in Shetland is a time for quiet contemplation and cozy comforts:

- **Hiking Among Fall Colors:** Follow the Whalsay Heritage Trail (Whalsay Heritage Trail, Whalsay ZE2 7TN) and witness ancient brochs shrouded in golden leaves. Hike the Fitful Head loop (Fitful Head, Unst ZE3 7TL) and feel the invigorating wind sculpt the landscape. Pack warm layers and sturdy boots, and let the crisp air paint your cheeks with a healthy blush.

- **Harvest Festivals:** Join the locals at the Scalloway Agricultural Show (Scalloway Agricultural Show, Scalloway Harbour, Scalloway ZE1 0XT) in October and celebrate the fruits of the land. Sample Shetland lamb pies, sip on local cider, and watch sheepdog trials showcase the incredible bond between farmer and canine. Immerse yourself in the island's traditions and soak in the genuine warmth of the community.

- **Pub Evenings by the Fire:** After a day exploring, step into a cozy pub like The Crafty Crow in Lerwick (The Crafty Crow, 58 Commercial St, Lerwick ZE1 0LA; +44 (0)1595 755020) and let the crackle of the peat fire fill you with warmth. Sip on a Shetland Red Ale, listen to local tunes, and share stories with friendly locals. Let the atmosphere wash over you like a Shetland blanket, wrapping you in comfort and good cheer.

12.3 Winter Landscapes & Northern Lights

The wind becomes a sculptor here, carving snowdrifts into fantastical shapes and etching tales of resilience on the landscape. The sea roars a deep song, churning with the fury of winter storms. And sometimes, if you're lucky, the heavens unfold like a celestial tapestry, adorned with the emerald and amethyst brushstrokes of the Aurora Borealis:

Winter Wonderland Walks:

Hike the Roekae Trail (Roekae Trail, Whalsay ZE2 7TN) as snow-dusted hills shimmer under a low winter sun. Follow the Mousa Broch trail (Mousa Broch, Mousa ZE2 9PU) and let the wind whip your hair as you stand awestruck before this ancient stone sentinel. Dress warmly, layer up waterproofs, and be prepared for changeable weather. The reward? Untouched landscapes painted in white, with the rhythmic roar of the ocean as your soundtrack.

- **Chasing the Aurora Borealis:** On clear nights, when the heavens dance with solar storms, the sky above Shetland ignites with the breathtaking Aurora Borealis. Head away from light pollution to sites like Skaw Road (Skaw Road, South Mainland ZE3 7TL) or Muness Castle and wait for the celestial show. Download an Aurora Borealis app to predict potential activity, pack a thermos of hot chocolate, and wrap yourself in warm layers. Patience and a dose of wonder are your most valuable companions.

- **Cozy Winter Pubs & Cultural Delights:** As the wind howls outside, seek refuge in a welcoming pub like The Mareel Bar in Lerwick (Mareel Bar, 53 Bridge St, Lerwick ZE1 0LA; +44 (1595) 756050) and warm your hands by a crackling fire. Sip on a Shetland gin hot toddy, savor Shetland lamb stew, and listen to tales of Viking lore whispered by the flames. Don't miss the Up-Helly-Aa fire festival in January (described in Chapter 11), where Shetland's Viking spirit erupts in a blaze of torches and revelry.

Beyond the Seasons:

While each season paints Shetland in its own unique hues, this island gem offers adventures year-round. Spring bursts with newborn lambs and the promise of warmer days. Festivals like the Scalloway Spring Fling in May celebrate the return of sunshine, while the hills echo with the calls of returning birds.

Know Before You Go:

Shetland weather is famously changeable, so pack layers for all possibilities. Sturdy boots are essential for outdoor adventures, and don't forget a swimsuit – hidden coves and sheltered bays beckon for an invigorating dip, even in winter. Public transportation is limited, so consider renting a car for maximum flexibility. Most importantly, come with an open heart and a thirst for adventure. Shetland isn't just a place; it's an experience waiting to unfold, woven with the threads of wind, sea, and stories whispered on the wind.

Chapter 13: Essential Information & Practical Tips for Adventurers

Ah, Shetland. The wind whispers promises of adventure, the waves beckon with tales of wild beauty, and the land stretches out like a tapestry woven with history and mystery. But before you dive headfirst into this island wonderland, let's pause, take a breath, and equip ourselves with the knowledge that will turn your Shetland odyssey into a saga worthy of Skaldic bards.

13.1 Getting Here & Getting Around

Reaching Shetland is an adventure in itself, a choice between two distinct, yet equally thrilling, options:

Soaring Through the Skies:

- **Direct Flights:** From London, Manchester, and Edinburgh, a quick hop aboard a Loganair plane deposits you in Tingwall Airport (Sumburgh Airport, ST21 EWX; +44 (0)1950 400011) in just over an hour. Expect to pay around £150-250 for a return flight, depending on the season and your booking flexibility.

- **Scenic Ferry Journeys:** From Aberdeen and Kirkwall in Orkney, NorthLink Ferries (northlinkferries.co.uk) whisk you across the North Sea aboard their comfortable vessels. The journey takes around 12-14 hours, but it's a mini-cruise in itself, with stunning coastal views and the chance to spot dolphins and whales. Prices start at around £60 for a one-way foot passenger ticket, and you can even bring your car for an additional fee.

Once you've arrived, navigating the islands is a breeze:

- **Buses:** Shetland's public bus network, operated by Stagecoach (stagecoachbus.com), connects Lerwick with most towns and villages. Buses run regularly during the day, but frequencies decrease in the evenings and on weekends. Fares are reasonable, starting at around £2-3 for a single journey.

- **Car Hire:** Renting a car gives you the ultimate freedom to explore at your own pace. Several car rental companies operate in Lerwick and Sumburgh, with prices ranging from around £30-50 per day. Remember, though, driving on the left-hand side of the road might take some getting used to!

- **Island Hopping:** For the truly adventurous, ferries connect the main islands of Mainland, Bressay, Whalsay, and Yell. Check timetables and book tickets online through Shetland Islands Council (shetland.gov.uk) or directly with the ferry operators. Prices vary depending on the route and season but expect to pay around £10-20 for a return foot passenger ticket.

Top Tip: Consider purchasing a Shetland Visitor Pass if you plan on doing a lot of island hopping or using public transport. This pass offers unlimited travel on buses and ferries for a specific period, saving you money and hassle.

13.2: Shetland's Finest Hotels

Serenity at Busta House Hotel: A Historic Haven Overlooking Busta Voe

Busta House Hotel:

Address: Busta, Brae, Shetland, ZE2 9QN, UK

Contact: +44 1806 522 506

Amenities: Restaurant, Bar, Free Wi-Fi

Website: www.bustahouse.com

Nestled on the shores of Busta Voe, Busta House Hotel stands as a historic retreat that seamlessly blends heritage with modern comfort. Dating back to the 16th century, this hotel exudes a sense of timeless elegance. The lush gardens, charming interiors, and sea views make it a perfect escape for those seeking tranquility.

The Experience:

As you enter the cobbled courtyard of Busta House, you're transported to an era where hospitality was an art. Check-in and take a stroll through the gardens, adorned with vibrant flowers and offering breathtaking views of the voe. The hotel's library, with its crackling fireplace, is a cozy spot to unwind with a book or savor a dram of local whiskey.

Local Highlights:

Explore the nearby Tangwick Haa Museum, just a 10-minute drive away, showcasing Shetland's history and maritime heritage. For dinner, indulge in the hotel's restaurant, renowned for its locally sourced ingredients. Try the Shetland Lamb Wellington (£24.95) for a culinary journey through the islands.

Tips for Guests:

- Reserve a sea-view room for an immersive experience of Shetland's coastal beauty.
- Take advantage of the hotel's packed picnic lunches when heading out for a day of exploration.

Coastal Luxury at Sumburgh Hotel: A Seaside Haven with Panoramic Views

Sumburgh Hotel:

Address: Sumburgh, Shetland, ZE39JN UK

Contact: +44 1950 460201

Amenities: Bar, Restaurant, Free Wi-Fi

Website: www.sumburghhotel.com

Perched on the southern coast of Mainland Shetland, Sumburgh Hotel offers a captivating blend of coastal luxury and rugged charm. With panoramic views of the North Atlantic, this hotel provides an ideal vantage point for witnessing the dramatic Shetland weather and the mesmerizing Northern Lights.

The Experience:

Arrive at Sumburgh Hotel and be greeted by the sound of crashing waves and the invigorating sea breeze. Check into a sea-view room to wake up to the sight of seabirds and, if you're fortunate, the dance of the auroras. The hotel's maritime-themed décor and comfortable amenities create a welcoming atmosphere.

Local Highlights:

Explore the nearby Sumburgh Head Nature Reserve, a haven for seabirds and a prime location for wildlife enthusiasts. For a taste of local flavors, head to the hotel's Cliftosha Restaurant. The Shetland Mussels in Garlic and Cream (£10.95) are a must-try.

Tips for Guests:

- Opt for a guided tour offered by the hotel to explore the nearby archaeological sites and natural wonders.
- Check the Aurora forecast and step outside in the evening for a chance to witness the Northern Lights.

Coastal Elegance at Shetland Hotel: Lerwick's Premier Accommodation

Shetland Hotel:

Address: Holmsgarth Road, Lerwick, Shetland, ZE1 0PW, UK

Contact: +44 1595 695515

Amenities: Restaurant, Bar, Gym, Free Wi-Fi

Website: www.shetlandhotels.com/Shetland/shetland.html

Situated in the heart of Lerwick, the Shetland Hotel stands as Lerwick's premier accommodation, offering a perfect blend of coastal elegance and urban convenience. With its modern amenities and proximity to local attractions, it's an ideal base for exploring the capital and its surroundings.

The Experience:

Check into the Shetland Hotel and appreciate its contemporary design and comfortable rooms. The hotel's central location allows for easy exploration of Lerwick's charming streets, shops, and historical sites. Unwind in the hotel's bar, known for its selection of local and international beverages.

Local Highlights:

Stroll along the Lerwick waterfront and explore the Shetland Museum and Archives, just a short walk away. For a taste of local seafood, dine at the hotel's Marlex Restaurant. The Shetland Salmon Fillet (£19.95) is a delectable choice.

Tips for Guests:

- Ask the hotel staff for recommendations on local events and festivals happening during your stay.
- Take advantage of the hotel's gym facilities to stay active during your trip.

13.3 Budgeting & Packing Wisely

Shetland's unpredictable weather demands careful planning, both in terms of budgeting and packing essentials for your journey.

Budgeting Tips:

- **Dining Out:** On average, expect to pay £15-£25 for a meal at a mid-range restaurant. Embrace local delicacies, and explore pubs for a more budget-friendly dining experience.

- **Transportation:** Car rentals range from £40-£80 per day, depending on the vehicle type and rental duration. Ferry tickets from Aberdeen to Lerwick start at £25 per person.

- **Activities:** Guided wildlife tours, such as puffin-watching, can cost around £30-£50 per person. Entrance to heritage sites, like Jarlshof, is approximately £6-£8.

Packing Essentials:

- **Clothing:** Shetland's weather is changeable, so pack layers. A waterproof jacket, sturdy walking shoes, and a hat are essential. Even in summer, a light sweater is advisable.

- **Outdoor Gear:** If you plan to explore nature reserves or hike, bring binoculars and a reliable camera to capture Shetland's wildlife and landscapes.

- **Travel Adapters:** Shetland uses the UK-style Type G electrical socket, so ensure you have the appropriate travel adapter for your electronic devices.

- **Local Currency:** While cards are widely accepted, having some local currency in cash is advisable, especially in more remote areas.

To make the most of your budget, consider self-catering options for some meals and explore local markets for fresh produce. Additionally, take advantage of free or low-cost activities, such as coastal walks and birdwatching, to immerse yourself in Shetland's natural beauty without breaking the bank.